Oxford Phonics World Readers

At the Bay

by Lynne Robertson

Illustrated by Michael Garland

OXFORD
UNIVERSITY PRESS

198 Madison Avenue
New York, NY 10016 USA

Great Clarendon Street, Oxford, OX2 6DP, United Kingdom

Oxford University Press is a department of the University of Oxford. It furthers the University's objective of excellence in research, scholarship, and education by publishing worldwide. Oxford is a registered trademark of Oxford University Press in the UK and in certain other countries

First published in 2013
2025
19

General Manager, American ELT: Laura Pearson
Executive Publishing Manager: Shelagh Speers
Senior Managing Editor: Anne Stribling
Senior Development Editor: Jennifer Wos
Development Editor: Diana Nott
Art, Design and Production Director: Susan Sanguily
Design Manager: Lisa Donovan
Designer: Jessica Balaschak
Electronic Production Manager: Julie Armstrong
Production Artist: Elissa Santos
Image Manager: Trisha Masterson
Image Manager: Joe Kassner
Production Coordinator: Christopher Espejo

ISBN:978 0 19 458910 9

Printed and bound in Great Britain by Bell and Bain Ltd, Glasgow

This book is printed on paper from certified and well-managed sources

The manufacturer's authorised representative in the EU for product safety is Oxford University Press España S.A. of El Parque Empresarial San Fernando de Henares, Avenida de Castilla, 2 – 28830 Madrid (www.oup.es/en or product.safety@oup.com). OUP España S.A. also acts as importer into Spain of products made by the manufacturer.

Words

Phonics words

bay	five	nine
bones	game	tail
cave	home	time
cute	June	way
dive	late	

Sight words

a	go	see	to
and	have	swim	walk
fin	I	that	we
fish	is	the	with
friend	it	they	
fun	look	this	

It is June.
We walk to the bay to swim.

I dive. I see five cute fish.

We have a game. I swim this way.

They swim that way.

This is fun.

We go to a cave.

We see nine bones.

Look! A fin and a tail!
Time to go!

We go with a friend.

It is late.
We go home.
Look! The fin and the tail!

Activities

A Match.

1. 

2. 

3. 

4. 

- bay
- cave
- five
- tail

B Look at the shapes. Write.

1\.

t ______ l

2\.

t ______ me

3\.

h ______ me

4\.

g ______ me

5\.

b ______

6\.

c ______ te

C Match.

1. We walk to the bay to swim.

2. We have a game.

3. We see nine bones.

4. We go with a friend.

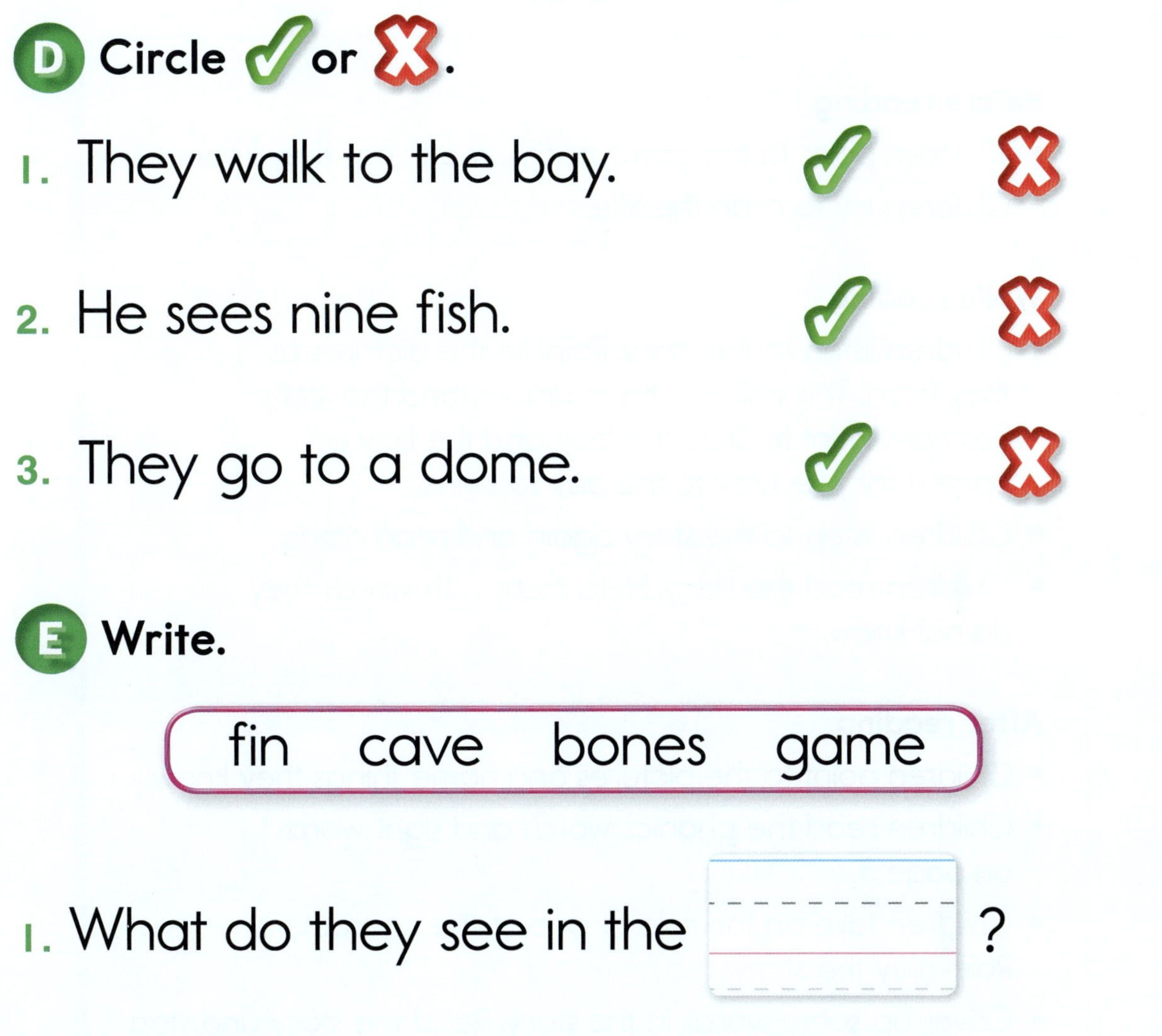

D Circle ✓ or ✗.

1. They walk to the bay. ✓ ✗
2. He sees nine fish. ✓ ✗
3. They go to a dome. ✓ ✗

E Write.

fin cave bones game

1. What do they see in the ______ ?
2. They see nine ______ and a ______ .
3. We have a ______ .

Notes

Before reading

- Children point to the cover and name things they know.
- Children try to read the title.

While reading

- Children listen to the story. Point to the pictures as they listen. This will help them understand the story. Example: Point to Dad, the boy, and the bay on page 4 for *We walk to the bay to swim.*
- Children listen to the story again and read along.
- Children read the story. Help them with words they do not know.

After reading

- Children point to the pictures and name things they know.
- Children read the phonics words and sight words on page 3.
- Children take on the role of one of the characters. Role-play the story.
- Cover up some words in the story. Read the story and stop at each covered-up word. Children say the missing word.
- Children do all the activities on pages 12–15. Check answers with the children.
- Children talk about the story. What did they like?